Poems That Bind

Evelyn Owens Kelly

Fulton Books
Meadville, PA

Published by Fulton Books 2023

ISBN 979-8-88982-289-9 (paperback)
ISBN 979-8-88982-290-5 (digital)

Printed in the United States of America

To my late mother, Leola Owens

Contents

Preface

This is a collection of poems dedicated to my late mother, Leola Owens (August 2, 1921–December 5, 2002). She was born and raised in Atlanta, Georgia. She wrote poems in the 1950s to help her get through some tough times. I kept some of the poems she wrote and put them together in this book.

Poems That Bind is a collection of writings that span three generations. The impact of her writings encouraged me through life. Her words transcend time. I was privileged to share her works with my children when they were younger. They were inspired to write poems of their own.

I have included some of my writings in this collection and those of my son, Armon Kelly, and my daughter, Bria Kelly. My writings reflect some of the more recent occurrences of our times. These are words of inspiration and encouragement.

Background

When I was a little girl in Atlanta, Georgia, we didn't have much. We were poor, but we didn't know it because we were healthy, happy, and had high self-esteem. I am the youngest daughter of eleven children.

My mother worked cleaning houses in the 1960s and 1970s.

When I was fifteen, I even went and cleaned a lady's house because my mother had to go and see about a sick relative. I had to take three buses to get to the lady's house, and when I got there, she was surprised to see a person so young. I told her that my mother had to go and see about a sick relative and that I was there to work in her place. Mrs. Leonard, the homeowner, let me in and told me what needed to be done. She had two young sons and said that I would need to prepare lunch for them because she would be out running errands. She looked at me and asked me if I wanted to do this for the rest of my life, and I told her I planned to go to college one day, but I wanted to make some money while my mother was out of town.

I proceeded to do the work as Mrs. Leonard had instructed.

At some point, her young sons informed me that they were hungry, and they asked me where was Leola (my mother). I told them that her name was Mrs. Owens and that I was her daughter and that I would prepare their lunch. I made grilled cheese sandwiches and tomato soup. I also made myself a grilled cheese sandwich. I cleaned up the dishes after lunch and finished my chores. I cleaned the upstairs bedrooms and bathrooms before lunch. I still needed to vacuum and dust.

At about 3:00 p.m., Mrs. Leonard returned home. She inspected the house and said that I had done a good job. She paid me $25 and took me to the mall to catch my bus to go back home.

My mother was so surprised when I called her and told her that I had gone to Mrs. Leonard's house. She couldn't believe it. She was happy and also sad because I told her I went out there to make money to buy food, and she knew she hadn't left much money.

No matter what my family went through, my mother always had a positive outlook. She completed the eleventh grade and quit school to get married and began having children. She told me that when times were tough, she would write poems to uplift her spirits. She also read these poems to her children. My siblings were much older than me. My mother had me and my younger brother much later in life. There were seven boys and four girls. Five of my brothers served in Vietnam back in the late '60s and early '70s. She told us that the military had a negative effect on them, and she would recite the poems she had written to encourage them.

My mother only had an eleventh-grade education, but she was very smart. She would help us with schoolwork, but most importantly, she helped us with our self-esteem. She would always tell us that we were somebody and that we could be anything we wanted to be. She would tell us not to let anybody tell us we weren't good enough. She encouraged us to hold our heads high and be proud of who we were. I was the only one of Leola's eleven children to go to college and then went on to get my master's degree. I am a retired superintendent of a small school district in Madison, Illinois. I am proud to say that I was able to bring my mother to my home before her death in December 2002.

My kids are grown, and when they were younger, I would read my mom's poems to them, and it encouraged them. They had to deal with different issues such as bullying and cliques. My mother's poems instilled a sense of pride and encouraged their self-esteem. They both finished college and are doing quite well for themselves.

We hear about bullying now and see the effects it has on our children and our schools. We have to love and embrace our children, build their self-esteem, and encourage them to talk with one another and resolve conflict in a peaceful way. We also have to model this behavior.

When I was a superintendent in the early and mid-2000s (I retired in 2016), I used to tell parents that we had to model the behavior we expected to see in our kids: we had to resolve conflicts peacefully, we shouldn't bully people, and we have to treat one another with respect. As I write these words today (2023), I think of our current political climate, and I pray.

Our world has been through a lot over the past few years. The pandemic placed a hush over us that we never saw coming, and when the world stood still and was shut down due to COVID-19, people were scared, and out of this fear came a sense of togetherness. Hundreds of millions of people died worldwide, and those of us who survived are trying to go back to a sense of normalcy.

Unfortunately, with that normalcy, the world is beginning to see mass shootings again, crime is on the rise, and so are mental health issues and suicides. I hope and pray that people can take time to appreciate that we're still here; we survived COVID-19. It was the most traumatic experience we've ever lived through.

Words of encouragement such as my mother's poems and other inspirational writings fill me with a sense of calm in this crazy world with its unpredictable weather.

I hope that the writings below will be as encouraging and uplifting to you as they have been to me over the years.

Mama's Poems

The poems that follow are poems my mother wrote back in the 1950s. These were her words of inspiration that helped her get through tough times. She also used these poems to help her children get through tough times. I have found them encouraging and uplifting over the years. I even read them to my children when they were younger to help them get through challenges. Sometimes in life we need inspiration and to be reminded of our inner strength and to renew our faith in a higher power. This is what my mother's poems have done for me.

Keep Going Ahead

If you are trying to reach the top,
sometimes you may almost drop.
Lift your head up; don't you stop.
You go ahead.
People might say you won't even pass;
don't ever think about that class.
If you try hard, you will succeed.
Just go ahead.
Sometimes the road might seem rough;
the going might get tough.
Take another start and say,
"I'm going ahead."
After you have reached your goal
and you are able to take control,
whatever your task be, do it well and just
keep going ahead.

My Prayer

(Leola Owens)

The worse I feel, the harder I pray.
I ask the good Lord each night and day
To help me along the way.
Protect me from all harm that may befall me so I won't stray.
As I travel upon this path,
Keep my feet pointed thy way.
When I open my mouth to pray,
Lord, stay with me day by day.

You've Got to Think High to Rise

(Leola Owens)

If you think you are beaten, you are
If you think you dare not, you don't
If you like to win but think you can't
It's almost a cinch you won't

If you think you'll lose, you're lost
For out in the world we find
Success begins with a person's will
It's all in the state of mind

If you think you are outclassed, you are
You've got to think high to rise
You've got to be sure of yourself
Before you can claim your prize

Life's battles don't always go
To the stronger or faster man
Because, sooner or later, the person who
Wins is the one who believes they can
You've got to think high to rise

Kids' Poems

The poems that follow were written by my son and daughter, Armon and Bria, when they were in elementary school. I used to read my mother's poems to them, and they would be inspired to write their own.

Over the years, things have been moved around in the house; some things were taken with them when they moved out. These are the only poems I could find.

Grandma

(Armon Kelly)

A grandma is not just someone who calls you sweetheart
she is someone with a warm and caring heart
A grandma is not just someone filled with many soft feathers
she is someone with many treasures
A grandma is not just a gift of love
she was sent from the beautiful stars above

God

(Armon Kelly)

God is good
God gives food
God is great
God gave me faith
God is bright
God gave me a special spark of light
God has power
God built me as a strong tower
As long as God makes a special day
Nothing will stand in my way

The Two Roads

(Armon Kelly)

When there are two roads to take
What choice will you make
The one to the east is the road to drugs
The one to the west goes on and on
The road to the east is full of holes
The road to the west is full of gold
So when you choose the best,
Remember, I'm headed for the west

Family

(Bria Kelly)

Families laugh, and families cry
they argue, fuss, and fight
but in the end, they'll be there for you
to help you do what's right

A family's love will fill your soul with warmth
and protect you from the cold outside
young people must respect their elders
because they will serve as your guide

No matter where life leads you
don't get lost in foolish pride
you only need look inside your heart
because that is where the family resides

They say blood is thicker than water
and with this, I must agree
because when I look around me
a beautiful family I see

Life's Journeys

The next set of poems expresses emotions that come with life's journeys. My daughter's poem was written when she finished college and moved out. She went through ups and downs with relationships, jobs, and life in general.

I've included some writings in this section as well because I too have gone through ups and downs in marriage, family relationships, and life in general, and so have some of my friends. I've shared my ups and downs with close friends and family; the poems are just ways to express the journey.

From Hell to Happy

(Bria Kelly)

We are responsible for our outcomes
Everything that has happened had to happen
Everything that will happen was already written
Nothing under the sun that is happening to you hasn't
occurred in history before

See the beauty in everything instead of the ugly
Remain positive even in negativity
Make peace with what you can't change
What we endure in life is meant to change/mold us
If not, we will repeatedly find ourselves in similar predicaments
Life is a journey: sometimes we go through hell to get to happy

When I Think About

(Evelyn Kelly)

When I think about all I've been through,
I ask myself, "Did all that really happen to you?"
Then a voice in my head says, "Yes, yes, it
did, and you made it through.
Your undying faith in God helped pull you through.
Don't you ever give up hope.
Don't you ever give up on you."
I have found a new sense of confidence and self-worth
When I think about what all God pulled me through.

Take It Back

(Evelyn Kelly)

Don't let anyone put you down and make you lose your self-esteem
Don't give them the satisfaction of seeing you like that
Take it back
Your self-esteem is what gives you the courage
to feel better, do better, be better
Take it back
If you've ever been cheated on, body-shamed,
Bullied or overlooked at work
You might feel bad because your self-esteem is hurt
It's natural, and it's okay to feel that way for a little
while, but then you remember who you are
And you begin to smile
Take it back
Remember you have people who love you;
most importantly, you love yourself
You've done good things; you've accomplished a lot
Don't let someone's negative actions, comments,
or behavior throw you off track
Take control of your life; regain your self-esteem
Take it back

Marriage Is a Journey, Not a Destination

(Evelyn Kelly)

Some people dream of getting married. At one time, it was considered the pinnacle of success in life. Once you get a decent job, the next step is to get married and have a family. One of the things you quickly learn is that marriage is a journey, not a destination.

It is filled with happiness and sadness, ups and downs, love and hate; and in the beginning, it can be so great.

As you journey together down this road, you begin to understand that it is the merging of bodies, minds, money, and souls and that one individual is no longer in control. You must learn to respect each other's opinions and compromise. Open communication is key; you can't keep secrets or tell lies.

As kids come along, they fill you with love and joy. You join together to raise the little girl or boy. As they grow older, you might drift apart. When people are selfish, they follow their mind, not their heart.

The evils and temptations of the outside world begin to take a toll: infidelity, alcohol, gambling, whatever it may be.

You learn that it's not a destination, but marriage is a journey.

I Had Such a Teacher

(Evelyn Kelly)

As I reflect on my inspirations in life, I can't help but include a teacher.

When I was in eighth grade, my mother cleaned house for a teacher; her husband was a successful lawyer. My mother would talk about me to this teacher and informed her that I would be entering the ninth grade in the fall and attending the high school where she taught. The teacher came by to meet me one day because my mother had told her so much about me. She told me that she would be looking for me when I got to high school.

When I entered Booker T. Washington High School, the oldest Black high school in Atlanta, Georgia, the school Martin Luther King Jr. attended, I looked Mrs. A up. Mrs. A taught in the business education program.

During my sophomore year, I included business education classes on my schedule and ended up in Mrs. A.'s class. She was the coordinator of the school's DECA program (Distributive Education Clubs of America). This program taught students job skills (résumé writing, application completion, mock job interviews, etc.)

By my junior year, I had earned enough academic credits, and I was able to take fewer classes. With Mrs. A.'s help, I obtained a job at a local bank. I took my academic courses in the morning and caught the bus to work in the afternoon.

There was a DECA district chairperson competition in Valdosta, Georgia, and Mrs. A. talked me into entering the competition. I had never spoken before a crowd of people, but I had to stand up in front of a large crowd and make a speech. When I finished, Mrs. A. told me she thought I had won. She said that she could see the look on the people's faces as I spoke, and she thought they were impressed. She was right; I did win. She was so proud.

When I graduated from college, I wasn't sure how my mother would get to Nashville from Atlanta because she didn't own a car. But I will always remember looking out of my dorm window and seeing this beautiful black Mercedes-Benz pull up to the dorm and my mother stepping out of the passenger side and Mrs. A stepping out of the driver's side. I cried tears of joy.

When I got married, Mrs. A. held the rehearsal dinner at her house, and she helped with the wedding party rehearsal.

We have kept in touch over the years. This teacher was very inspirational to me; she, like my mother, helped me to believe in myself and helped me believe I could do anything. I am so thankful that she has been a part of my life, and I am thankful that I had such a teacher.

Embrace Your Roots

(Evelyn Kelly)

Embrace your roots no matter where you're from
Because part of who you are today was shaped by your dad or mom
Some of us started from humble beginnings,
whether working class or poor
Those humble beginnings helped shape our
character and made us strive for more
They taught us to respect ourselves and others,
and they taught us to hold the door
Embrace your roots and the manners that
you were taught back then
Words like "please" and "thank you" were so common
Now we rarely hear them; I can't remember when
We learned that we had to work hard in
life, and we did so with pride
We didn't give up; we couldn't give up even if we tried
Embrace your roots because they helped to make you strong
We look around today and wonder where work ethics have gone
There seems to be a lack of good customer service;
sometimes, selfishness gets in the way
They're here today and gone tomorrow, workers just don't stay
Social skills have suffered; we see it every day
We have to encourage positive human
interaction; at least, we have to try
We can model good behavior by saying "please,"
"thank you," "hello," and "goodbye"

If only we could teach people today the
things we were taught back then
They might approach life differently; those kind,
courteous, and respectful ways would
Return once again
Embrace your roots because they made you who you are
The things we were taught back then have carried us far

A Salute to Black Panther: Wakanda Forever

This poem is a salute to the movie *Black Panther*, which takes place in a fictitious country called Wakanda.

The movie was first released in February 2018. There was a part 2 of this movie released in November 2022. However, the first movie was eye-opening, mythical, and magical, and its lead character, Chadwick Boseman, was an outstanding actor. Unfortunately, Mr. Boseman died in August 2020, leaving many of his fans heartbroken. His work lives on in *Black Panther* and other movies he made prior to his death.

Wa—What?

(Evelyn Kelly)

The first *Black Panther* movie made its
nationwide debut on February 16, 2018,
and the world went Wakanda crazy.
Wa—what? You ask. That's right, Wakanda:
a fictitious African village.
Everyone knows that it was fake, but the beautiful depiction of
this place in the movie made us dream of the possibilities, the
what-ifs, the wishful thinking of the beautiful, mythical place,
Wakanda.

Wa—what? You might ask.
Wakanda, the land of beautiful people, superior
technology, precious metal, and that powerful
purple flower.
Wa—what?
Wakanda, a place that just might give our people a sense
of pride, self-worth, self-respect, dignity, and power.
A place that just might help our people appreciate
our natural beauty and make us stand tall.
A place that might make our brothers and sisters
love themselves—hair, skin, features, and all.
Wa—what?

Wakanda, a place that might encourage our people to stop killing each other senselessly, which is our greatest downfall.
Wa—what?
Wakanda, a place that had us all in awe.

*****

Disney's Marvel Studios director, Ryan Coogler, and an outstanding cast introduced the world to the fictitious African village of Wakanda on the big screen on February 16, 2018, and we are forever grateful.

Our hearts were saddened by the death of Chadwick Boseman on August 28, 2020. Chadwick Boseman starred as the Black Panther, T'Challa, the King of Wakanda. A second *Black Panther* movie, *Wakanda Forever*, was released on November 11, 2022.

Be Healthy, Be Happy

This next section is to encourage people to eat healthy and take care of themselves. We all come in different shapes and sizes. Whatever our size or body type, it is important that we do our best to take care of ourselves. We cannot judge others for having surgery to enhance their looks, self-esteem, and beauty. However, we can encourage people to adopt a healthy lifestyle, incorporating food and exercise to improve their health and well-being.

Food Is the Enemy

(Evelyn Kelly)

I see people sick and about to die; you must realize why
You cannot eat and drink everything you see once you
understand that this processed food is the enemy
Processed foods will ruin your health over time
You need to eat right and exercise and have a healthier goal in mind
Fruits, vegetables, baked chicken, and baked
fish can help you, and so can green tea
Because food, this processed food, is the enemy
Drink purified water; eat fruit, vegetables, and nuts;
walk and exercise; you must do these things
regularly
We suffer from high blood pressure, diabetes, and high cholesterol
The side effects from the medicines they prescribe takes a toll
We can be healthy if we strive to be, because this food
This processed food is the enemy

We Are So Beautiful

(Evelyn Kelly)

We are so beautiful, you see; why can't we let ourselves be?
We are doing so much to make ourselves look pretty
because we are unhappy with what we see.
We think we're fat, so we get lipo; honestly, that's not the way to go.
We think we're too thin, so we get fat stuffed in.
We enhance our boobs, our lips, our thighs,
and our butts; my goodness,
What's the matter with us?
We are so beautiful, you see; we all have unique beauty.
Be proud of how you look.
Don't let fictitious beauty standards have you shook.
Our beauty is rare and unique because we are so beautiful, you see.
Learn how to be happy and accept your individual beauty.

The World Stood Still

This last section is about the day the world stood still, the day the coronavirus took this world by storm, the day this virus brought the world to a total standstill, the scariest time in my life. This virus ripped through the United States and other countries around the world like nothing we had ever seen in modern times. We all knew what it felt like to be terrified and scared. I will never forget this fear and the feeling of total helplessness.

Where Are the Birds?

(The Coronavirus 2020)
(Evelyn Kelly)

On Tuesday, March 31, 2020, I looked out my kitchen window into the backyard and wondered, *Where are the birds?*

My husband refilled the bird feeder the day before, but still no birds. This was week 2 of us being sheltered in since the coronavirus took hold of the world.

What did the birds know? Where did they go?

*****

Today is Thursday, April 2, 2020. The world is at a standstill due to the onset of the coronavirus. My last day working at Lane Bryant was Saturday, March 14, 2020.

On Sunday, March 15, 2020, my daughter was baptized at Faith Community Bible Church in Jennings, a small community in St. Louis, Missouri. I made grocery store runs (at Target and Walgreens) early to stock up on food, water, toiletries, medicine, Lysol, hand sanitizers, and other essentials. Businesses, schools, and stores were shut down; only essential workers were allowed to go to work (healthcare personnel, police, firefighters, grocery store staff, etc.).

My daughter worked at a bank and was frustrated because they would not allow her and other staff to work from home even though they talked with customers over the phone and used their computers.

On March 31, 2020, I told her to tell her boss she would not be returning to work until this virus subsided.

We didn't understand it. People were getting sick and dying. My sister-in-law, Hazel, had sheltered in like everyone else. However, her husband would go to the grocery store. At first, he thought she had passed out; but when she got to the hospital, he found out she'd had a stroke. She didn't have any of the usual symptoms of COVID-19 (cough, fever, loss of smell, taste, etc.). She died a few days after being taken to the hospital.

When Lane Bryant closed in March of 2020, my coworker Martha sent us videos of how to fight the virus. The store reopened in June 2020. Martha called and texted me to ask if I was returning. I told her I had decided not to return.

In July, I didn't hear from her. I drove by the store and didn't see her car on the lot. I decided to go in with my mask and gloves on to ask about her. I was told that she had contacted COVID-19 and was in ICU on a ventilator.

In August 2020, Martha died of COVID-19. I was heartbroken.

This virus had taken the world by storm; stores were closed. Restaurants, movie theaters, major league sporting events, concerts, any and all events with potentially large and small gatherings had been shut down. The coronavirus was highly contagious and potentially deadly. It killed millions of people around the world. It was like we were living in the twilight zone. We were required to wear masks and gloves when we went out. We had to social distance, and we could not come within six feet of one another. There were markings on the floors in stores to direct people where to stand so that we would remain at a six-foot distance. We couldn't touch one another. People were afraid to talk to one another. We could only talk with our masks on and only at a safe distance. Some stores installed protective glass shields to protect employees from any potential spread. Again, it was like we were living in the twilight zone.

One day, as I was getting in my car after completing a supply run, I looked around and saw people in masks and the look of despair in their eyes. I began to cry. I got in my car, and I cried, and I prayed. I asked God to place a shield of protection around us and help us get through this unthinkable crisis.

This virus not only affected us physically but it also took a toll mentally. The physical isolation was too much for some people to handle; suicide rates increased. Kids could not go to school. The schools had to resort to virtual learning. People could not gather in church. Churches had to resort to virtual services. Again, we were living with something that none of us understood. We tried to be brave, but most of us were scared as hell. This was a world that none of us recognized, none of us could imagine. It was like the twilight zone.

In December 2020, vaccines were introduced to help protect people against the virus.

As of March 2023, the world has regained a sense of normalcy. The coronavirus, or COVID-19, as it is referred to, is still present; however, the vaccine has helped increase immunity. Masks are no longer required, people are traveling, outdoor and indoor events are being held, and schools and churches have resumed services.

We move forward with cautious optimism because we know COVID-19 is still out there; people are still getting the virus, it's just in fewer numbers, and the survival rate has greatly improved. Some of us still wear masks. We look twice at people when they cough in public and don't have on a mask and don't cover their mouths.

The birds did return; they were never really gone. In my fear, I just couldn't see them.

About the Author

Evelyn Kelly is a retired school superintendent who was born and raised in Atlanta, Georgia. She attended Fisk University in Nashville, Tennessee, where she obtained her bachelor's degree. She later obtained her master's degree from Southern Illinois University in Edwardsville, Illinois. She met and married her husband, Clarence Kelly, and they raised two kids, Armon and Bria Kelly. Evelyn obtained her superintendent certification from Western Illinois University in Macomb, Illinois. Evelyn enjoys reading, cooking, and working in her flower garden.